A SHORT BIOGRAPHY OF FRANKLIN DELANO ROOSEVELT

A SHORT BIOGRAPHY OF
Franklin Delano Roosevelt

Karen Roth

Carlisle, Massachusetts

A Short Biography of Franklin Delano Roosevelt

Series Editor: Susan DeLand
Written by: Karen Roth

978-1-944038-27-4

FRONT COVER: *Franklin D. Roosevelt,* 1947
Frank O. Salisbury (English, 1874–1962)
Oil on canvas
White House Collection/White House Historical Association

BACK COVER: *President Franklin D. Roosevelt Delivering Fireside Chat #6,*
September 30, 1934
Still photograph
Courtesy of the Franklin D. Roosevelt Presidential Library & Museum

Published by Benna Books
an imprint of Applewood Books, Inc.
Carlisle, Massachusetts 01741

To request a free copy of our current catalog
featuring our best-selling books, write to:
Applewood Books, Inc.
P.O. Box 27
Carlisle, Massachusetts 01741
Or visit us on the web at: www.awb.com

10 9 8 7 6 5 4 3 2 1
MANUFACTURED IN THE UNITED STATES OF AMERICA

HOPE WAS THE HALLMARK of Franklin Roosevelt's life. Hope drove him to lead America through a great economic crisis and to victory in an incendiary global conflict. Hope made a debilitating disease into a mere backdrop for an accomplished career.

Franklin Delano Roosevelt was born January 30, 1882, at Springwood, an estate in Hyde Park, New York, in the Hudson River Valley. Born into a blue-blood family, he was called Master Franklin by the family's servants. The only child of James Roosevelt and Sara Delano, Franklin was the center of his mother's world and the apple of his father's eye. His mother poured all her love and energy into her only son. She was domineering but instilled in Franklin a strong sense of self-confidence. James passed on to his son his good humor and his sense of duty toward those who were less fortunate.

When Franklin was a child, President Grover Cleveland patted him on the head and said that he wished for the boy's sake that he would never become president.

Franklin was tutored at home, receiving few visits from children his own age. He grew up comfortable and communicative with adults, not children. When Franklin was eight, his father had a heart attack. Squire James, as everyone on the estate called him, faced a steady decline but lived another decade.

Young Franklin developed interests in bird-watching, photography, maritime collections, and stamp collecting. He took the stamp collection all the way to the Oval Office, where it helped him unwind from the stress-filled days. As president, he created and designed postage stamps in support of New Deal policies. Eighty-five countries have created commemorative stamps in his honor.

By the time of his death, FDR had collected 1.2 million stamps.

His mother reluctantly sent her son away to school when he was fourteen, two years after most of his classmates had entered Groton School, a prestigious boarding school in Massachusetts. Franklin's tutors had prepared him well academically, but he did not have the social skills to be popular with his peers.

Groton was an academically challenging school, and dormitory life, where the day started with an icy shower, was a rude awakening for the pampered Franklin. He had trouble relating to his classmates. Discipline was rigorously enforced, and the headmaster, Reverend Endicott Peabody, encouraged bullying as a method of toughening the students. It was a rough transition for a boy raised with attention, privilege, and indulgence. Nevertheless, Franklin wrote home that he was "getting along great with the fellows," hiding his feelings from his parents. Franklin earned excellent grades at Groton and did so well in his entrance exams to Harvard that he was admitted as a sophomore. While he was at Harvard, his father died. Now Franklin was the sole focus of Sara's attention. Distraught at the death of her husband, she left Hyde Park and moved to Boston, near Franklin.

A close relative said that Sara was an indulgent mother who would not let her son call his soul his own.

At Harvard, Franklin pursued a degree in history and became managing editor and then president of the *Crimson,* the school newspaper. Becoming more socially confident, Franklin joined many clubs, with his heart set on becoming a member of the exclusive Porcellian Club. Both his father and his fifth cousin Teddy Roosevelt had been members. An unknown person blackballed him from membership. Not being "punched by the Porc" was a lingering humiliation. After Harvard, Franklin moved on to law school at Columbia University in New York City.

Hiding his feelings from his possessive mother had become second nature, and he kept his courtship of young women secret. Franklin and Eleanor Roosevelt were distant cousins who saw each other occasionally in childhood. While attending Harvard, he ran into her on the train to New York and they spent the time in rapt conversation. Her intelligence and philosophical conversations impressed him, and they began dating. Eleanor was unlike the other vapid debutantes in his circle. Given his own serious side, hidden behind a charming facade, he believed he would do well with her by his side. She was the most interesting woman he knew, an opinion he held throughout his life. When Franklin proposed, Eleanor accepted.

Entries in his diary tell of dating a woman named Eleanor.

Although they were from the same prestigious background, their childhoods were dramatically different. He was the son of an adoring family, but her childhood was riddled with pain and loss. Eleanor's father, Elliott, was a dissolute drunk. Her mother, Anna Hall, was a capricious beauty whose only daughter was not. She cruelly called Eleanor "Granny." Because

Elliott was eventually institutionalized after he impregnated one of the maids.

of her mother's coldness, Eleanor idolized her father, despite his behavior. Once, when Elliott took Eleanor and three dogs for a walk, they stopped outside the Knickerbocker Club. He told her to wait with the dogs while he went inside. Six hours later he emerged, falling-down drunk.

Diphtheria claimed the lives of her mother and her brother Elliott when Eleanor was eight years old. Her father, in and out of sanitariums for alcoholism and unable to care for his surviving children, sent them to their grandmother's care.

At fourteen, Eleanor was sent to Allenswood Academy in England, where she found caring and respect in a seventy-year-old teacher, Mademoiselle Marie Souvestre, who guided Eleanor to excel at everything she did. Eleanor absorbed the lessons of open-mindedness, social consciousness, and independent thinking. "Whatever I have become since had its seeds in those three years of contact with a liberal mind and a strong personality," said

Eleanor of her teacher. This education shaped the young woman who accepted Franklin Delano Roosevelt's marriage proposal.

An astonished and resistant Sara asked them to wait a year before making their engagement public.

Franklin's mother tried to keep them apart, taking Franklin on a Caribbean cruise. Meanwhile, Eleanor taught immigrant children at a settlement house. When he returned, Franklin visited Eleanor at the tenements, where a child fainted. Franklin, deeply affected, carried the child home. "My God," he told Eleanor, "I didn't know anyone lived like that."

In love with Eleanor, Franklin was undeterred by his mother's disapproval. When Uncle Ted, as Eleanor called him, heard of the engagement, he sent Franklin a note:

"Dear Franklin,

We are greatly rejoiced over the good news. I am as fond of Eleanor as if she were my daughter; and I like you, and trust you and believe in you. . . . You and Eleanor are true and brave and I believe that you love each other unselfishly; and golden years open before you. May all good fortune attend you both, ever.

Give my love to your dear mother.

Your aff. cousin,
Theodore Roosevelt."

Eleanor and Franklin Roosevelt were wed on March 17, 1905. Their witnesses were President Theodore Roosevelt and First Lady Edith Roosevelt. Eleanor was the favorite niece of Theodore Roosevelt, Elliott's brother. Franklin idolized Teddy and once said that he was the greatest man he had ever known. Franklin modeled his political career after Teddy's, succeeding in an uncanny parallel series of positions: New York state legislator; assistant secretary of the navy; governor of New York; and president of the United States. Although Teddy was a Republican and Franklin a

When Franklin discovered that he needed glasses, he chose the same style and material as Teddy's.

Democrat, they respected and admired each other's ideals.

Returning from their honeymoon, the young couple discovered that Sara had purchased a house for them in New York. She furnished and decorated it and designed an adjoining residence for herself. Eleanor wept and Franklin did not comprehend why. For years, Franklin sat at one end of the dining table and his mother at the other. Eleanor sat in the middle with the children. Franklin never curtailed his mother's dominating presence.

Franklin and Eleanor wanted a large family and had six children. Sadly, their son Franklin died in infancy. The Roosevelts had four surviving sons and a daughter. Motherhood mystified Eleanor, who'd had such poor role models in her parents. She turned to her mother-in-law for help. Her daughter Anna remembered her grandmother dressing them, teaching them manners, and showering them with "consistent, warm, spontaneous love." Sara's darker side appeared when she

Their children were Anna, James, Franklin (who died in infancy), Elliott, Franklin Jr., and John.

would whisper to them, "Your mother only bore you, I am more your mother than your mother is."

Franklin worked at a law firm to support his growing family. His associates were dreaming of becoming partners. He said he wanted to be president of the United States. No one laughed. After all, there was a Roosevelt in the White House.

Franklin ran for state senator of New York in 1910. No Democrat had won that seat in thirty-two years, but FDR rode the tide that swept Democrats to victory nationwide, winning the seat. The *New York Times* reported: "Senator Roosevelt is less than thirty. He is tall and lithe. With his handsome face and his form of supple strength he could make a fortune on the stage and set the matinée girl's heart throbbing with subtle and happy emotion. But no one would suspect that behind that highly polished exterior the quiet force and determination that now are sending shivers down the spine of

Tammany's striped mascot." However, Frances Perkins (later FDR's secretary of labor and the first woman to be appointed to a cabinet post) recalled a more arrogant demeanor. FDR sometimes made a snobbish impression, cocking his head back and sticking his nose in the air. True to expectations, he did take on the Tammany Hall bosses and voted for many reform bills.

Tammany Hall, a powerful political society, had a ferocious tiger for a mascot.

When it was time to run for reelection, Eleanor and Franklin had typhoid fever and could not campaign. Louis Howe became FDR's strategist. Howe was small in stature and self-deprecating, humorously answering the phone, "Medieval Gnome here," and often calling his employer "Beloved and Revered Future President." He was a trusted adviser until the day he died and always felt free (unlike others) to tell his boss when he thought FDR was acting like a "damn fool." Howe campaigned for Franklin and secured his reelection to the state senate.

Franklin was invited to Democratic

President-elect Woodrow Wilson's inauguration. Secretary of the Navy Josephus Daniels found Franklin impressive and offered him the position of assistant secretary. FDR jumped at the chance. Teddy Roosevelt had been assistant secretary and Franklin loved all things navy. Franklin and Eleanor rented Teddy Roosevelt's sister Bami's home in Washington, D.C.

Franklin was thirty-one years old, the youngest assistant secretary of the navy.

Franklin was impatient with his boss's slow pace. While Secretary Daniels was on tour, Franklin took full advantage of being in charge. The United States had entered World War I, and FDR felt it was imperative to strengthen the navy. Roosevelt proposed implementing the North Sea Mine Barrage, a complex plan to lay hundreds of thousands of nets and explosive mines between Scotland and Norway to curtail the submarine threat. Daniels vetoed the proposal, but FDR went over his head and secured approval from President Wilson himself.

Eleanor hired Lucy Mercer as her

social secretary to navigate the unfamiliar ways of Washington, D.C. However, the war freed Eleanor from the political social whirl in a subdued Washington, and she focused her energies on the Red Cross and the Navy Relief Society.

Lucy was twenty-two years old and came from a well-connected family that was now financially strapped.

In the summer of 1918, Franklin went on a naval inspection tour to Europe and contracted pneumonia on the way home. While Eleanor was nursing him back to health, she unpacked his suitcases and discovered a packet of love letters from Lucy Mercer. Eleanor was devastated. She remembered, "The bottom dropped out of my own particular world," and she was forced, she said, "to face myself, my surroundings, my world, honestly for the first time."

Eleanor offered Franklin his freedom, but Sara told him that if he left his wife and five children she would cut him off financially and he would never inherit the Hyde Park estate. Moreover, Lucy Mercer was Catholic and prohibited from marrying a divorced man. Franklin

Louis Howe chimed in that if he chose divorce, it would end his political career.

chose to stay with his wife and children. Their marriage was forever altered, yet years later, their children testified to the love and respect that remained between them.

FDR returned to Europe with President Wilson in 1919 to oversee the demobilization of the American Navy, and would accompany the President on his return voyage after the Paris Peace Talks. The president had an initial draft of the Treaty of Versailles, which included Wilson's hope for a League of Nations. The president traveled the United States promoting the league, fell ill, returned to the White House, and had a massive stroke. First Lady Edith Wilson hid the extent of his disability from the public, including Congress. Despite Wilson's warning that "the United States must go in or it will break the heart of the world," the Senate rejected the treaty.

FDR never forgot seeing his hero on the porch of the White House in a wheelchair after his stroke, unable to mutter but a few words and heartbroken by the vote.

Franklin resigned as assistant secretary of the navy to run as the vice presidential candidate on the ill-fated James Cox ticket for the 1920 election. He crisscrossed the country campaigning and learning about the American people. Franklin knew that Cox was a long shot, but Franklin took the opportunity for exposure, honing his political skills.

FDR returned to New York at the beginning of 1921, a force to be reckoned with in the Democratic Party. Roosevelt hired Missy LeHand as his personal secretary. She became indispensable in his political career and in his life. She was his secretary, companion, and political gatekeeper. She took care of the household accounts and his personal correspondence. Missy was the de facto chief of staff during Roosevelt's presidency.

In August 1921, the family vacationed at their summer home on Campobello Island in Canada. Franklin and Eleanor loved being there. He could romp and play and sail and hike with their children, just as he had done as a child. On August 10, Franklin took Eleanor

There was no electricity but an abundance of natural beauty.

and their sons James and Elliott on a sailboat ride. When they saw a small forest fire, he led everyone ashore to put it out. Then he sailed home, went swimming in a pond two miles away, and raced his sons home—a typical day, until tragedy struck. Complaining of fatigue and nausea, Franklin retired early. The next morning, he couldn't get out of bed. The local doctor misdiagnosed the symptoms. As the days went by the disease spread through his whole body. He couldn't walk; he couldn't hold a pen. On August 25, 1921, Dr. Robert Lovett, an expert in the field, diagnosed infantile paralysis, also known as polio. There was no known cure or treatment for polio, which was often a death sentence at the time. Survivors were condemned to a significantly disabled life, suffering physical agony and social stigma.

Eleanor gave Franklin round-the-clock care, but by September it was still unclear if Franklin would be able to sit up in a chair. Eleanor said that the only time she broke down in tears in front of him was when he called cheerfully to his family, "Look what I can do." He was able, though in great pain, to slide on his belly to the door in case of fire.

Franklin had a fear of fire, having seen, as a toddler, his Aunt Laura Delano burn to death when an alcohol lamp exploded.

Though he worked toward a full recovery, it became clear that Franklin would not regain the use of his legs. To head off a serious depression, he went to Florida and rented a houseboat. Away from his mother, wife, and children, he could mourn the loss of his legs and its implications.

Sara wanted to take her son back to the family estate in Hyde Park. Eleanor contradicted her formidable mother-in-law. Although Franklin's legs were withered, she knew that idleness would wither his soul. Louis Howe helped Eleanor keep the Roosevelt name in the public eye by coaching her to attend and speak at political events. Franklin worked on the slow, painful recovery of his health. Polio had not thwarted his political ambitions.

In his search for a cure, FDR went to Warm Springs, Georgia, "to take the waters." Here he could swim and exercise in the water with more fluidity and less pain. Franklin turned the dilapidated former resort into a polio rehabilitation center and hired professionals. It cost two-thirds of his fortune to renovate, but Warm Springs became a haven for polio patients from all over the world, who came to the center for physical therapy. This energized Franklin. He led exercise classes, encouraged frightened patients, and lost self-consciousness about his own withered limbs. Determined to take power over this disease, Franklin designed metal braces for his legs. True to his nature, he would make the guests laugh and lead them in games. They were braced by his hopeful spirit.

The guests loved Franklin and called him "Rosie."

Al Smith, governor of New York and the Democratic presidential candidate, asked Franklin to give the nomination speech at the Democratic convention in 1924. Franklin agreed, though it required him to walk to the podium on crutches. Four years later, in 1928, he once again made the nomination for Smith. By this time he had mastered the two-step walk taught to him by a physiotherapist in Warm Springs. This meant having the dead weight of his legs braced by ten pounds of steel and leaning heavily on someone's arm while forcing one half of his body forward at a time. He repeatedly practiced going to the podium with his son Jimmy. When the time came, Roosevelt made his way to the platform, grasping Jimmy's arm so painfully it made his son want to cry out, but father and son bravely smiled at the crowd. Jimmy became a fixture next to his father from that moment forward, through all the terms of FDR's presidency.

The New York *Herald Tribune* called FDR "the foremost figure on floor or platform."

Franklin ran for governor of New York in 1928. When Al Smith was asked why he suggested that FDR, a possible rival, replace him as governor of New York, Smith replied that Franklin would be dead in a year. FDR campaigned for governor through all sixty-two counties of New York. This grinding schedule was deliberate, illustrating that he was up to the job. In 1928, at the apex of the Roaring Twenties under the Republicans, the Democrats were going to have a difficult time. On election night, assuming defeat, Franklin and Eleanor left Democratic headquarters long before midnight. Sara stayed for the final results. When her son won at 4:00 A.M., Sara could only order milk to celebrate because of Prohibition.

After the stock market crash of 1929 and the onset of the Great Depression, FDR's record as governor of New York was one of reform and innovation based on the necessities of "social duty." The economy was in a downward spiral, with collapsing banks, foreclosed homes, and millions of people unemployed. FDR set up the country's first state commission to establish reliable jobless figures, established unemployment insurance, and created the Temporary Emergency Relief Administration, providing relief for the jobless. Because he was willing to act

The perceived paralysis of the Hoover administration's response to the national crisis was in stark contrast to FDR's dynamic leadership.

in this time of adversity in New York, FDR was nominated for president on the 1932 Democratic ticket.

Franklin's physical trial transformed him. Once he had been arrogant; now he was humbled, but not defeated. He learned empathy through his ordeal. Labor Secretary Frances Perkins said, "There had been a plowing up of his nature. The man emerged completely warm-hearted, with new humility of spirit and a firmer understanding of profound philosophical concepts." He was ready to lead a nation in crisis.

On November 8, 1932, Franklin Delano Roosevelt defeated Herbert Hoover to become the thirty-second president of the United States. Initially the crowds were bleak and despairing, but a wave of hope swept through the people when Franklin was sworn in and presented his inaugural address.

The Republican-leaning *Chicago Tribune* praised FDR's speech's "dominant note of courageous confidence."

"Let me assert my firm belief that the only thing we have to fear is

fear itself—nameless, unreasoning, unjustified terror which paralyzes needed efforts to convert retreat into advance."

The crowds cheered wildly. Almost half a million letters arrived at the White House the next week. Within hours of the inauguration, FDR had his entire cabinet sworn in to begin working immediately. In the first hundred days of the administration (the yardstick by which other presidents have been measured ever since), fifteen major bills signed by FDR were passed by Congress. The New Deal was born through the Emergency Banking Act, the Agricultural Adjustment Administration, the establishment of the Federal Emergency Relief Administration and the Civilian Conservation Corps, and many more actions that renewed the country's optimism.

FDR began speaking directly to the people through the radio, reassuring families in their living rooms. These "fireside chats" continued throughout his presidency, and Americans felt a personal connection to their president. The progressive programs continued. The Civilian Conservation Corps was joined by the Works Progress Administration (WPA), the New Deal's signature job program. The Truth-in-Securities Act imposed the first federal regulation on the stock market, followed by the Security and Exchange Commission, established in 1934. Social Security and unemployment insurance were instituted by law in 1935. Part of the upper classes objected mightily to these reforms. When Sara refused to pay her Social Security tax, FDR secretly paid it for her.

FDR supported the arts through the Federal Art Project and the WPA.

In 1936, FDR was reelected to a second term by a landslide. In his stirring inaugural speech, he said, "We have come far from the days of stagnation and despair . . . [yet] I see one third of a nation ill-housed, ill-clad, ill-nourished."

The specter of the Nazis overtaking Europe loomed when France fell in June

The American people as well as Congress were reluctant to enter another European conflict after World War I.

of 1940. By July, FDR was convinced that the country would need a strong and proven leader to face the horrors of Hitler. He won a third term in the Oval Office knowing it meant preparing for war. Britain stood alone against Germany and Italy, so FDR initiated the Lend-Lease Act to send supplies to England and China. On December 29, 1940, in a fireside chat known as the "Arsenal of Democracy" speech, Roosevelt convinced America of the necessity of devoting resources to aid the Allied Powers without entering the war. This began the country's march away from isolationism. Franklin believed that if Great Britain were conquered, the Axis powers (Germany, Japan, Italy) would control Europe and Asia, and the Americas "would be living at the point of a gun."

The surprise attack by the Japanese gutted the United States Navy of 20 ships and 300 airplanes. Nearly 2,500 lives were lost.

The following December, while Japan's representatives were speaking of diplomacy and peace in Washington, D.C., the Japanese imperial forces bombed Pearl Harbor, Hawaii. On December 8, 1941, FDR addressed both houses of Congress:

"Yesterday, December 7, 1941—a date which will live in infamy—the United States of America was suddenly and deliberately attacked by naval and air forces of the Empire of Japan. . . . I ask that the Congress declare that since the unprovoked and dastardly attack by Japan . . . a state of war has existed between the United States and the Japanese Empire."

One hour later, Congress declared war. Acutely aware that the United States was the last remaining hope of the free world, Franklin projected confidence and optimism: "The militarists in Berlin and Tokyo started this war. But the massed, angered forces of humanity will end it."

FDR's brilliance as a leader in World War II was his ability to see how one decision affects another. General George Marshall admired this talent. Roosevelt had named him chief of staff of the armed forces when World War

When being briefed about the war in the Pacific, FDR astonished his generals with his knowledge of the islands—knowledge he gained from his stamp collection.

II began in 1939. FDR admired and valued Marshall's candor and they both became more effective leaders in this worldwide crisis. They assigned talented and seasoned generals to the field to fight the mightiest war machine that the world had ever known. In a fireside chat in 1941, FDR said, "We are going to win the war and we are going to win the peace that follows."

When he visited a naval hospital for sailor amputees, FDR chose to appear in his wheelchair, offering himself as proof that their lives were not over.

The war raged on, with Allied troops landing in France on D-day in June 1944. The war took its toll on FDR's health; he developed heart trouble. Nevertheless, he won a fourth term as president in 1944. His inaugural address was a single page, delivered in a very subdued ceremony befitting a country at war. Eleven weeks later, knowing that victory was on the horizon, he retreated to Warm Springs for some much-needed rest. On April 12, 1945, he complained of an intense headache. He died of a cerebral hemorrhage that afternoon. He was sixty-three. Lucy Mercer was at his side.

Americans and the world were stunned. When Eleanor was told in Washington, she sent a telegraph to their four sons, all of whom were on active duty. Eleanor went to Georgia to accompany her husband's body on the train back to Washington, where she was joined by her daughter Anna. The train slowly wound its way north; thousands of mourning Americans lined the route.

A poverty-stricken man standing close to the tracks as the train carrying FDR's casket went by was crying. When asked if he knew the president, he said "No, but he knew me."

FDR's endurance and struggle with polio had rebuilt the relationship between Franklin and Eleanor. She became his eyes and ears and trusted access to the outside world. Throughout his presidency, she was his preeminent adviser on domestic issues, and together they brought about a social and economic revolution that altered the relationship between the government and the American people. This powerful political partnership fostered a nobility of the American spirit. The press had such respect for FDR that in the twelve years of his presidency, he was rarely photographed in his wheelchair. They shared, for the sake of the country, what has been called "his splendid deception."

When the rest of the world was engulfed in World War II and Britain stood alone, the relationship between FDR and Winston Churchill solidified a lifeline that helped to save civilization as we know it. Churchill said of FDR: "He is the truest friend; he has the farthest vision; he is the greatest man that I have ever known."